Quotes

Of

Passion

PassionPoet

Robert R. Gibson

An

Erotic Empire

Book

Editing / Book Layout by

Passionate Words
Editing Services

(IG @passionate.words.editing246)

Dedication

This book is dedicated to all those who are in love with love, in love with words, or specifically, in love with the words of **Passion**, the poet and author of the books EROTIC, OFFERING and SEDUCTION. If you have not yet experienced these soul searing words, delve into Quotes, and be exposed to the words of

Robert R Gibson, the *Passion Poet*.

Acknowledgements

I want to thank all my loyal fans that have stuck with me and my work over all these years. This book was the third in my collection, first published as an ebook in 2015. I had intended for it to become a paperback book for years, but never worked on it until I had a run-in with Amazon and all my books were taken down (who knew you weren't supposed to create a new account? Long story - if you want to hear it you can contact me via my socials. Nevertheless, it left me with an opportunity to work on it since I had to put the other books up anyway.

I want to also acknowledge all those who are lovers and lovers of poetry. This book is for you. If you happen upon this book when searching for Valentine's Day gifts - THIS IS THE ONE FOR YOU. *Smile*

Introduction

"How do I love thee? Let me count the ways..."

"A rose by any other name would smell as sweet..."

"Romeo, Romeo, wherefore art thou, O Romeo..."

These quotes are quite famous for any student of either literature or love. The first quote is from Elizabeth Barrett Browning, and the last two are from the great William Shakespeare himself.

Do you want to drop a morsel of sweetness into your lover's ear? Do you want to ignite their passions with a well-placed verse? This book achieves the same as the quotes above with snippets of longer poems written by Robert R Gibson, the PassionPoet, as well as small potent love verses called 'Wordshines.'

The term 'Wordshine' was coined by the object of Robert's affection while he was trying to court her by dropping a short freestyle poem into her electronic ear (he was using BlackBerry Messenger at the time) every morning, which was kept up for approximately three months. She said that it was like a burst of sunshine in her inbox using words, so she started calling them 'wordshines.'

Near the end of the first month, she asked if he was keeping the poems and storing them - which, prior to this, he had not. The joy of creating and having her smile was his only reward. However, at her insistence, he kept the next two months of work in a file. Some of them are now in this volume.

This book is a potent addition to Cassanova's arsenal. In it are droplets of literary gold that have been panned from the river of Passion's words. The mix of snippets and wordshines comes together to form a gold mine of sensual and romantic treasure that will be valued for all time!

CONTENTS

As my thoughts copulate with yours

And our conversation, now joined, starts in earnest and explores

The inner workings of each other's psyche

As we each get to understand how the other thinks ....

– Conversation

Your aura intoxicates me

Leaves me bobbing and weaving

trying to stand upright

on waves of undulating

emotions.

*I could stay wrapped in your arms forever till heaven sent for me –
then I'd beg them not to part us, 'cause eternally separated from you
would be the purest hell. Pulling out of your arms is always hard.*

– From The Heart

When we touch, my heart grows roots

Extending into your soul,

drawing sustenance from your essence.

Assimilating affirmation through osmosis,

Your touch feeds me.

— Hug

I love you
Love your smile, your laugh
Love the path my eyes
take across your curves
Love the energy your release
makes me weak in the knees
mix of sensuality and peace
that you carry with ease....
You're the Goddess Divine
How I wish you were mine
Treasure you for all time ...
but for now I'll distill
all my longing to this
potent elixir:
"I LOVE YOU."

For I have always loved you.

Your spirit finds mine over the span of several lifetimes;

We join each other over and over again.

In every age I search until I find you,

And we become one.

-- Inseparable

The secret's out

my heart is yours

kneeling before you

my soul pays homage

And, as we mesh into each other -

So close the casual observer couldn't tell us apart -

I thank the Universe that I have found you...

— *Inseparable*

My heart reaches out and kisses yours

Love pours out and fills my soul

till my tank is full and my day can start

But I leak

So I reach for your heart's oil can

and kiss you again tomorrow.

Open up for me

Sweet pink petals peeking cheekily

Lips curved in a smile

Molten desire like beads of sweat

Dripping down

Between folds of skin

— *Invocation*

Heart skips merrily down thought's path

Happily playing hop-scotch with desire

whenever my mind's eye gazes

mesmerized

at the beauty that is you

Smile rises above dismal cloud

banishing depression with rays of light

Our eyes meet

Sky as bright as noon

Your smile kisses my heart gently

my soul melts into putty

for you to shape at will

As we join together

two bodies

molded forever

into one soul

I realize finally

that our intimacy

heals completely

and we

once broken

become whole.

— Intimate

23

Your beauty arouses my muse

sensuality excites pen's muse

my heart speeds up

and I write

verses flow out

with all my might

Reluctant to pull away

we stand in the forever

between one second and the other

— Kiss Me

Thoughts of you are an oasis of calm

in the middle of a tsunami of busy-ness

I anchor my heart to your smile and rest

and watch the world flash by

through the window.

There is nothing new under the Sun

everything has already been sung or put to verse

but that doesn't stop my heart from singing your praises

doesn't stop my soul from penning rhymes

— Lost

Love is

Hearts constructed from same mould -

Ice melts water rises into vapour

Same substance

Different forms

Souls connected across eternity, time

Warps into meaningless void

— *Love Is*

My heart: a cup

overflows

you pour in beauty

every time I see

your smile

... wanna hold you close

Till hearts intertwine ...

Till I am yours

And you are mine with

Genuine intimacy...

Until we find the ultimate connection -

We merge until our two becomes, on

Closer inspection, one complete whole: ...

– Make Love to Me

Your beauty arrests me for loitering

as I stand immobile, staring

hand-cuff me, I'm not moving

lead me away, read my rights; I'm drooling

as I look into your eyes

I seek to enter the Sacred space:

The place of birth,

Of gestation;

My adoration is palpable - physical - sacrificial ...

So I do not come empty handed.

I bring everything I am to the house of worship -

The place where Goddess dwells,

— Offering

Kiss me

let earth fade

blurring perception

till all I sense

is your love

Staring deeply into my soul through your eyes,

I see ripples of our connection in our reflection.

Your pupils dilate as we consummate our love in our gaze.

— *Reflection*

n

I want to trace your lips with my finger

eye stare intense and linger

ing; passion aroused, red hot

molten and searing

branding your seal upon my

heart

Like the vine called love, I want to grow into you

And have you grow into me

Until the only separation existing

Is between this stanza

And the next.

— *Seduction*

I wish I could take you in my arms

And kiss you

Just once

And in that kiss would be all my desire

All the fire bottled up in me

That I can't release easily...

– Self Discovery

My heart caresses yours

tender touches drive away

pain of angry words

my kiss soothes soul's pain

You're not alone

So, it's been ordained....

I want to strip you -

Shame dropping like

your blouse

slowly peeling off

shoulders...

Boulders of

embarrassment

rolling away

as I stare at your breasts,

inviting me to touch.

– Strip You

When I first saw you, the earth stood still

My heart paused in the eternity between seconds

My breath stopped, I couldn't breathe...

– When

Banish chill wind of lonely night

touch me, light passion's fire

let's warm up in heated embrace

stoked with fiery kisses

Let me paint you into a work of art,

Chipping away at resolve with every stroke,

Carving out a masterpiece of

mutual manifestations of bliss,

Transferring the glimmer of anticipation

To actuality's solid form.

– Work of Art

Fingers locked

joined at the heart, we walk

two lives, one heartbeat

four eyes, one gaze

two bodies, one soul

two halves, one whole

Intimately connected

No more disjointed

You and I

Flying towards the horizon

— Invocation

In the still of the night

my heart longs to hold you tight

mould together until sunlight

can't pass between, try as it might

to break this bond that feels so right

I...

Wanna smell your arousal

Rising

Rising like incense burning

At the altar of Flaming Desire

— Sensual

I get high off you

As scent lingers

Heartbeat quickens

Desire sparked

— Inhale

As I speak, my words stimulate your mind -

Caressing each curve with nuances

Licking your thoughts' ear lobes with sweet somethings

That make your body tingle

—Conversation

You make me want to get vulnerable.

Make me want to peel off the layers of my soul and

Expose myself wholly to you -

— Vulnerable

If I didn't believe

in the Divine

I would change my mind

The second I fell

into your striking

eyes

One glance at your beauty and all control is lost;

I must come to you at any cost -

— Come

Seductive stares lock, earth stands still;

Nature holds breath as

Sizzling tongues spark molten heat

— Urge

So know, my love,

That really

There is more to you than you realize

And what I see with my eyes

Makes me want to explore

Learn more

And be a part of your

Self-discovery.

— Self-Discovery

Dawn brings thoughts of you

whispering quietly through my mind

tiptoeing so as not to wake

sleeping libido

I want to tickle you with my tongue -

Or rather, my voice -

As my choice of words brings joy

And makes you laugh

— *Letters*

Mind not attentive

Thoughts slip their leash

And run straight to you.....

Creativity signs your name

Calligraphy-style across my heart.

Diamond smile glitters across full lips,

Stripping me of speech

Like earth stripped of light at solar eclipse.

Heart tips hat, greeting

For every fleeting second I get to see your face.

I want to get to know you

— **Attraction**

Lingham stretching

reaching

longing

for intimate yoni

conversation

How do I love you?

I can't count the ways!

My love grows stronger

With every second, minute -

As hours stretch into days!

Each heartbeat, each breath,

Each morning as sun's rays

Break over horizon

– How do I Love You?

I steer around the curves with skill,

Still looking for the end of the road.

My final destination- your soul.

-- Letters

Other Books by PassionPoet

The quotes featured in this book are snippets taken from three of the published poetic anthologies by Robert R.Gibson, The PassionPoet - **Erotic**, **Seduction** and **Offering**. In order to read the poems these snippets were taken from in their entirety, please purchase the other books.

About The Author

Robert R. Gibson is a lover of words, both spoken and written. He was born and lives in his native Barbados, is married and has four beautiful children between him and his Queen Felicia. He is most known for his sensual and erotic work, but he writes on various topics; his most famous saying is "Passion isn't always about sex." He intends for your interactions with his work - either on the stage or in written word - to be an INTENSE experience.

www.ingramcontent.com/pod-product-compliance
Lightning Source LLC
Chambersburg PA
CBHW040200160726
48006CB00014B/1838